IMPERATIVE OF SOFTWARE TESTING:

THE POST OFFICE HORIZON SCANDAL

First edition. April 23, 2024.

Written by Julian Cambridge.

Note from the author

A defect is something the user doesn't want.

Introduction

The Post Office Horizon Scandal is one of the most significant legal and technological controversies to have occurred in the UK, deeply impacting the lives of numerous postmasters across the country and raising serious questions about the reliance on computer systems in the justice system. It revolves around the Horizon system, an IT system introduced by the Post Office in 1999. This software was intended to manage all aspects of Post Office transactions, including accounting and stocktaking.

Background of the Scandal

The core of the scandal lies in the fact that, from the early 2000s onwards, numerous Post Office workers, many of whom were sub-postmasters running post office branches, were accused of theft, fraud, and false accounting based on discrepancies reported by the Horizon system. These discrepancies often manifested as apparent shortfalls in cash or stock, which the software indicated were missing from various branches. As a result, hundreds of sub-postmasters were prosecuted, with many receiving prison sentences, being financially ruined, or suffering severe damage to their reputations.

Initial Discovery and the Role of Software

The initial discovery of the issues with the Horizon system came to light when affected sub-postmasters began to come forward, reporting that they were being held accountable for losses that they strongly believed they had not caused. Despite their claims, the Post Office continued to rely on the accuracy of the Horizon system, dismissing concerns raised about software errors and insisting that the discrepancies were the result of criminal activities by the branch staff.

However, further investigation and technical scrutiny eventually uncovered that the Horizon system was indeed flawed, prone to bugs and errors that could generate false financial shortfalls. These software glitches wrongly indicated that money was missing, leading to the unjust accusations against the postmasters.

The role of the Horizon software in this scandal highlights the critical issues of reliability and trust in computerised systems used for financial and legal decision-making. It also brings to attention the need for adequate oversight, rigorous testing, and transparent error reporting mechanisms in such systems to prevent similar tragedies from occurring in the future.

The uncovering of the Horizon system flaws led to a series of legal battles, culminating in the Court of Appeal quashing many of the convictions against the sub-postmasters, acknowledging that they were wrongfully charged based on unreliable evidence from the flawed software. This acknowledgment and the subsequent public inquiry into the matter have sparked widespread debate about the accountability of large institutions and the human cost of technological errors.

The Author

Julian Cambridge was born in London, UK.

- M.Sc. Business Computing
- B.Sc. (Hons) Computing with Business

Julian founded Golden Agile Solutions to supply IT consultancy activities to clients.

- Accredited Kanban Trainer (AKT, KMP, TKP)
- Certified Scrum Professional (CSM, CSPO, A-CSM, A-CSPO, CSP-SM)
- ICAgile Authorized Instructor (Agile Fundamentals, Agile Product Ownership, Agile Testing, Business Agility)

The Post Office Horizon Scandal

Testing governance

In the Post Office scandal, the level of access that software testers had to LIVE (production) environments isn't publicly detailed in the reports and discussions surrounding the scandal. However, the scandal itself highlighted significant failings in software testing, error handling, and overall management of the IT system. This system wrongly accused several sub-postmasters of theft, leading to wrongful convictions, financial ruin, and in some tragic cases, suicides.

Given the implications of the scandal, we can discuss what practices and processes should have been done differently in a general sense, focusing on software testing and quality assurance (QA) best practices that could potentially have mitigated such issues:

1. Rigorous Testing in Non-Production Environments: Before any deployment, it's crucial to conduct thorough testing in environments that mimic the production (LIVE) environment as closely as possible. This includes unit testing, integration testing, system testing, and acceptance testing to catch and fix bugs early.

2. User Acceptance Testing (UAT): Involving actual users or user representatives in the testing process can highlight usability issues and misunderstandings about how the software will be used in real-world scenarios.

3. Error Handling and Logging: Implementing robust error-handling and logging mechanisms would allow for the detection and investigation of issues without automatically attributing discrepancies to human error. This can help distinguish between genuine user errors, system errors, and issues that require further investigation.

4. Audit Trails: Maintaining comprehensive and tamper-evident audit trails that record actions and changes can help in troubleshooting and providing evidence for investigations. Transparency in transactions and operations is key in systems handling financial or sensitive data.

5. Escalation Processes: Establishing clear processes for escalating and handling anomalies detected by the system or reported by users. This includes mechanisms for reporting suspected bugs or issues without fear of reprisal.

6. Independent Review and Testing: Periodic reviews and testing by independent third parties can help identify issues that internal teams may miss or underestimate. This is crucial for systems that have significant legal or financial implications.

7. Continuous Monitoring and Feedback Loops: Implementing continuous monitoring of the system in production, along with feedback loops where issues can be reported, tracked, and addressed promptly.

8. Ethical Considerations and Stakeholder Communication: Ensuring that all stakeholders, especially those directly impacted by the system (e.g., sub-postmasters), are informed about how the system works, its limitations, and what to do in case of discrepancies.

The Post Office scandal serves as a stark reminder of the catastrophic effects that can result from a failure to adhere to rigorous software testing and quality assurance standards, especially in systems that significantly impact people's lives and livelihoods.

Creating 50 specific test cases for the Horizon software directly tied to the post office scandal involves both functional and non-functional aspects, aiming to identify the types of errors that could lead to wrongful accusations, like those seen in the UK Post Office scandal. Here's a structured approach to generating these test cases:

Functional Test Cases

1. Transaction Processing Accuracy: Verify that all types of transactions (e.g., sales, refunds) are accurately recorded.
2. End-of-Day Balance: Ensure that the end-of-day balance calculation matches the sum of the day's transactions.
3. Data Synchronisation: Test that transaction data is correctly synchronised between the local branch system and the central system.
4. Transaction Editing: Confirm that any authorised modifications to transactions are correctly updated and audited.
5. Error Logging: Check whether all system errors are logged with detailed information for troubleshooting.
6. User Access Rights: Verify that users can only access functions and data permissible by their role.
7. Authentication Mechanisms: Test login/logout processes and authentication measures to prevent unauthorised access.

8. Backup and Recovery: Ensure that backup procedures capture all necessary data and that recovery can be performed without data loss.
9. Data Integrity: Confirm that transactions are not corruptible or alterable by system malfunctions or unauthorised actions.
10. User Error Handling: Check how the system handles user input errors (e.g., invalid transaction entries).

Non-Functional Test Cases

11. Performance under Load: Test system performance under high transaction volumes to ensure it remains responsive and accurate.
12. Stress Testing: Evaluate how the system behaves under stress or when resources (e.g., memory, disk space) are low.
13. Usability: Assess whether the UI/UX is intuitive for users of varying skill levels.
14. Security Penetration Testing: Conduct penetration tests to identify vulnerabilities to hacking or unauthorised access.
15. Audit Trail: Verify that the system maintains a robust and tamper-proof audit trail of all transactions and system access.

16. Data Encryption: Check the encryption of sensitive data both at rest and in transit to prevent unauthorised access.

17. Compliance: Ensure the software meets all relevant postal and financial regulations and standards.

18. Disaster Recovery: Test the system's ability to recover from catastrophic failures without data loss.

19. Network Failure Handling: Examine the system's response to network interruptions, including data resilience and synchronisation after recovery.

20. Software Update Process: Verify that updates do not disrupt ongoing operations or alter existing data inaccurately.

Scenario-Based Test Cases

21. Incorrect Balance Reports: Simulate scenarios where transaction data is inaccurately reported, potentially implicating a user in fraud.

22. Hardware Failure: Test the system's resilience and data integrity in the event of hardware malfunctions.

23. Power Interruption: Determine the system's ability to recover from sudden power losses without data corruption.

24. Multi-User Access Conflict: Assess how the system handles concurrent access or data entry by multiple users.

25. Remote Access Risks: Evaluate security risks associated with remote access and ensure data is protected.

26. Transaction Rollback: Test the ability to rollback transactions in the case of errors without affecting overall data integrity.

27. Legacy System Integration: Verify that the software correctly integrates and communicates with existing postal systems and databases.

28. Data Migration Accuracy: Ensure that data migration processes from old systems to Horizon do not result in data loss or inaccuracies.

29. Custom Reporting: Test the accuracy and customisability of reporting features for financial auditing and operational needs.

30. Fraud Detection Mechanisms: Evaluate the effectiveness of built-in fraud detection algorithms and reporting.

Extreme and Edge Case

31. Maximum Transaction Volume: Test the system's handling of transactions at the maximum volume limit.

32. Minimum Transaction Amounts: Check how the system handles transactions of very low value to ensure accuracy.

33. Uncommon Transaction Types: Test less common or complex transaction types for accuracy and correct reporting.

34. International Transactions: Assess the system's ability to accurately process and convert foreign currency transactions.

35. Date and Time Manipulation: Evaluate the system's resilience to incorrect date or time changes, which could affect transaction recording.

36. Rapid Succession Transactions: Simulate transactions entered in rapid succession to check for system overloading or errors.

37. Manual Override Functions: Test the integrity of manual overrides by authorised users and the corresponding audit trail.

38. Recovery from Database Corruption: Assess the system's ability to detect and recover from database corruption scenarios.

39. Interest and Fee Calculation: Ensure that any calculations for interest or fees are performed accurately and recorded correctly.

40. Long-term Data Retention and Retrieval: Verify the system's ability to store, manage, and retrieve transaction data over long periods accurately.

User Experience and Accessibility Test Cases

41. Ease of Navigation: Assess how easily users can navigate the software to perform common tasks.
42. Accessibility Features: Test the software's compliance with accessibility standards, catering to users with disabilities.
43. Multi-language Support: Verify the accuracy and usability of multi-language support within the software.
44. Help and Documentation: Check the availability and helpfulness of in-software documentation and support features.
45. Feedback Mechanism: Evaluate the effectiveness of the system's mechanism for collecting and addressing user feedback or reports of inaccuracies.

Additional Considerations

46. Integration with Postal Hardware: Test compatibility and integration with postal-specific hardware (e.g., printers, scales).
47. Batch Processing: Ensure accurate processing and reporting of batch transactions.
48. Customised Access Levels**: Verify that customised user access levels function as intended, preventing unauthorised operations.

49. System Update Rollbacks**: Test the ability to rollback system updates in case of issues without losing data.
50. External Audit Interface**: Ensure the system provides necessary interfaces and data access for external audits without compromising data security.

Each of these test cases would be carefully designed to uncover any potential faults that could lead to incorrect accusations, financial discrepancies, or operational failures, similar to those experienced by the Post Office due to the Horizon software issues.

The Horizon System: Origins and Operations

Development and Deployment of the Horizon System

The introduction of the Horizon system marked a transformative phase in how the Post Office conducted its business, moving towards more digitised, efficient operations. It was designed to handle a wide array of tasks, including transaction processing for mail, financial services, and government services, as well as managing the accounting and stocktaking for each branch. The Horizon system was rolled out across thousands of Post Office branches, becoming an integral part of daily operations by the early 2000s.

The Post Office Horizon Scandal

The role it played in post office operations

The Horizon system played a central role in the operations of the Post Office, enabling a standardised platform for the execution and management of transactions across the entire network of branches. It allowed for real-time tracking of sales, stock levels, and financial transactions, providing a comprehensive overview of the operational health of each branch.

One of the key features of the Horizon system was its ability to automate many of the traditional paper-based tasks, thereby reducing the potential for human error in financial calculations and record-keeping. It was also intended to simplify the auditing process, giving the Post Office's central management a powerful tool to monitor branch performance and ensure compliance with operational standards.

In theory, the Horizon system was a leap forward in terms of efficiency and control, designed to benefit both the Post Office and its customers. It allowed for quicker transaction times, improved accuracy in handling finances, and provided a robust framework for expanding the range of services offered at Post Office branches.

However, the reliance on the Horizon system also meant that any flaws or inaccuracies in its operation could have far-reaching consequences. As it turned out, the system was not as infallible as believed, leading to the misreporting of financial transactions and, ultimately, to the wrongful accusation of many sub-postmasters. Despite its intended role as a tool for improving Post Office operations, the Horizon system became the focal point of a scandal that highlighted the risks associated with deploying complex IT systems without sufficient oversight and accountability measures in place.

Early Warning Signs of the Horizon system in the post office scandal: Ignored or Misunderstood?

The Horizon system's deployment across the UK's Post Office network was accompanied by early warning signs that were either ignored or misunderstood by management and the IT team responsible for the system. These early indicators pointed to underlying issues that would later culminate in a scandal affecting many sub-postmasters.

First Instances of Discrepancies

Almost immediately after the Horizon system was put into operation, reports of discrepancies began to emerge from various Post Office branches. Sub-postmasters, who were responsible for the individual branch operations, reported unexplained financial shortfalls in their accounts, which the system indicated. These were not isolated incidents but appeared across a range of different locations and under varying operational circumstances.

The discrepancies often involved significant sums of money, leading to confusion and distress among the sub-postmasters. Many of them could not reconcile their physical cash and stock with the figures reported by the Horizon system. The expectation was that such a sophisticated system would reduce or eliminate accounting errors; however, the reality was starkly different, with errors appearing more frequently and on a larger scale than under the previous, more manual systems.

Responses from Management and IT

The response from Post Office management and the IT team overseeing the Horizon system ranged from dismissive to outright accusatory. Initially, these entities showed a tendency to trust the infallibility of the computerised system over the accounts and experiences of the sub-postmasters. When discrepancies were reported, the common response was to attribute them to human error, misconduct, or lack of understanding of the new system on the part of the sub-postmasters.

Instead of conducting a thorough investigation into the possibility of system errors, management often pursued disciplinary measures against the sub-postmasters, including fines, repayments of supposed shortfalls, and, in some cases, legal action leading to convictions for fraud and theft. This approach not only ignored the early warning signs but also contributed to a culture of fear and silence, discouraging others from coming forward with their experiences.

The IT team responsible for the Horizon system appeared to be either unaware of the scale of the discrepancies or unwilling to acknowledge any potential flaws in the software. Reports suggest that bugs and glitches were either minimised or not properly addressed, with updates and fixes implemented without fully understanding their impact on the system's operation.

Conclusion

The early warning signs of the Horizon system's failings were both ignored and misunderstood, leading to a significant scandal. The over-reliance on technology, combined with a dismissive attitude towards those experiencing the system's flaws first hand, underscored a systemic failure in management and oversight. It was only after years of legal battles and the ruin of many lives that the true extent of the system's problems was acknowledged, leading to a reassessment of how large IT projects should be managed and monitored, especially within critical public service infrastructure.

Lives in the Balance: The Impact on Sub-postmasters in the post office horizon scandal

Personal Stories of Affected Sub-postmasters

The scandal touched the lives of hundreds of sub-postmasters, who were often the heart of their communities. Many were respected local figures whose lives were turned upside down by the accusations. One poignant example is that of a sub-postmaster who ran a small, community-loved post office. After the Horizon system showed a shortfall, they were accused of theft and faced criminal charges. Despite their insistence on their innocence, the legal battle that ensued led to severe financial strain, loss of reputation, and profound emotional distress. Some sub-postmasters were even wrongfully imprisoned, their personal and professional lives irrevocably damaged.

Legal Toll

Legally, the scandal led to an unprecedented overturning of convictions. After years of fighting, it was recognised that the faults in the Horizon system were responsible for the discrepancies, not the sub-postmasters. The legal battles were lengthy and costly, with many forced to fund their defence, leading to financial ruin for some. The reversal of these convictions has been one of the largest miscarriages of justice seen in the UK, highlighting significant failures in the legal and postal systems.

Financial Toll

The financial impact on affected sub-postmasters cannot be overstated. Many spent their life savings on legal fees trying to clear their names. Others were forced to pay back supposed shortfalls to the Post Office, leading to debt and bankruptcy. The loss of their businesses and livelihoods had long-term financial repercussions, not just for the individuals but for their families as well.

Emotional Toll

The emotional and psychological toll on those accused was devastating. The shame, stress, and stigma of being falsely accused of a crime led to broken families, mental health struggles, and in some tragic cases, suicide. The fight to clear their names and the eventual recognition of their innocence came too late for some, leaving a lasting mark on their lives and the communities they once served.

In conclusion, the Post Office Horizon scandal is a stark reminder of the devastating impact that systemic failures can have on individuals. The personal stories of affected sub-postmasters bring to light the considerable legal, financial, and emotional toll experienced by those caught in the scandal. It underscores the importance of accountability and the need for systems that protect rather than harm individuals serving their communities.

Unravelling the Truth: Investigations and Findings in the post office horizon scandal

External Analyses and Investigations into the Horizon System

Initial Accusations and Dismissals:
- The problem began in the early 2000s when numerous sub-postmasters faced wrongful accusations of theft, fraud, and false accounting based on discrepancies reported by the Horizon system. Many were fired, financially ruined, prosecuted, or even jailed based on these inaccuracies.

Independent Investigations:
- Early whistle-blowers and individual investigations faced strong pushback from the Post Office, which steadfastly defended the Horizon system's integrity. However, persistent concerns led to a series of independent investigations:

- Second Sight, a forensic accounting firm, was commissioned to conduct an independent review. Its reports, although initially restricted and later released in full, highlighted significant issues with the Horizon system, including bugs, errors, and a lack of reliability in its transaction data.
- Parliamentary Inquiries: The UK Parliament's Business, Energy and Industrial Strategy Committee also scrutinised the matter, calling for accountability and revisions in Post Office operations.
- Criminal Cases Review Commission (CCRC): Many convictions were referred to the CCRC, which in turn highlighted potential miscarriages of justice, leading to appeals in higher courts.

Key Findings and Acknowledgments of System Failures

Acknowledgment of Flaws:
- After years of denial, the Post Office admitted that the Horizon system was indeed flawed, contributing to the financial discrepancies that led to the wrongful accusations against sub-postmasters.

Legal and Judicial Acknowledgments:
- A landmark ruling in December 2019 by the High Court in a group litigation order involving hundreds

of sub-postmasters found that the Horizon system was indeed responsible for the anomalies that led to the wrongful accusations. This judgment acknowledged the system's failures and the Post Office's aggressive legal stance against sub-postmasters.
- In 2020 and 2021, some wrongful convictions began to be overturned by the Court of Appeal, acknowledging the miscarriages of justice that occurred.

Government and Post Office Response:
- The UK government initiated an inquiry into the scandal, aimed at uncovering the extent of the wrongdoing and ensuring such failures are not repeated.
- The Post Office has publicly apologised to the affected sub-postmasters and agreed to compensation settlements, although debates about the adequacy of these settlements continue.

The Broader Impact:
- The scandal has led to a fundamental re-evaluation of the Post Office's cultural, operational, and governance practices.
- It has also raised significant questions about the oversight of public institutions and the reliance on

complex IT systems without adequate error checking or accountability mechanisms.

The Horizon scandal underscores the necessity of transparency, accountability, and rigorous independent scrutiny in the operation and management of significant national infrastructure, particularly when it directly affects individuals' lives and livelihoods.

The Role of Software Testing in the post office horizon scandal: What Went Wrong?

Examination of the Software Testing Protocols Used by the Post Office

The Horizon system was developed by Fujitsu, and as part of its implementation, software testing protocols would have been a foundational requirement to ensure integrity, reliability, and accuracy in transaction processing. Effective software testing involves multiple stages, including unit testing, integration testing, system testing, and acceptance testing, all of which are designed to identify and rectify errors throughout the development and deployment phases.

However, in the case of the Horizon system, it became progressively clear that the software testing protocols either were not sufficiently rigorous or failed to account for real-world operational complexities. The software exhibited bugs and errors that led to financial discrepancies. These discrepancies were erroneously attributed to human error or intentional misconduct by the sub-postmasters.

Analysis of How and Why These Measures Failed

1. Insufficient Testing and Verification: It appears that the Horizon system was not subjected to adequate real-world testing scenarios that accurately reflected the diverse operations of post office branches. A rigorous software testing protocol would have identified and addressed the system's inability to handle certain transaction types without generating errors.

2. Lack of Transparency and Accountability: The Post Office and Fujitsu were criticised for a lack of transparency over the system's issues. For a long time, they denied the presence of software bugs that could cause discrepancies, placing the blame on the sub-postmasters instead. This denial hindered any constructive investigation into the software's reliability.

3. Ignoring User Reports: Reports from sub-postmasters about unexplained discrepancies were

often dismissed. This reaction suggests a failure in the post-deployment software testing and maintenance protocols, which should include continuous monitoring and feedback mechanisms to capture and correct system faults.

4. Legal and Institutional Obfuscation: The legal battles faced by the sub-postmasters highlighted a significant failure in the judicial and institutional understanding and scrutiny of software-based evidence. There was a lack of critical examination of the Horizon system's reliability, which allowed the software's failings to translate into wrongful convictions.

5. System Complexity and Error Handling: The complexity of the Horizon system, combined with poor error handling and reporting mechanisms, made it difficult to trace and understand the root causes of discrepancies. Effective software testing should encompass strategies for managing complexity and ensuring clear, actionable reporting of errors.

The Post Office Horizon scandal is a sobering example of how inadequate software testing, combined with institutional intransigence and lack of transparency, can lead to severe consequences. It underscores the importance of rigorous, transparent, and user-informed testing and maintenance protocols for complex software systems, especially those with significant financial and legal implications.

Lessons Learned from the post office horizon scandal: Best Practices in Software Testing

This case highlights critical lessons and underscores the necessity of best practices in software testing. Here are detailed insights into lessons learned and the successful implementation of thorough testing protocols:

1. Introducing Robust Software Testing Methodologies

- Implement Comprehensive Testing Strategies: Embrace a multitude of testing techniques, including unit, integration, system, and acceptance testing to cover all possible scenarios.

- Automate Where Possible: Use automated testing tools to repeat testing tasks, ensuring consistency and covering a broader array of test cases.

- Rigorous Quality Assurance (QA) Processes: Establish strong QA processes that actively involve both testers and stakeholders in identifying and resolving issues early in the development cycle.

- Continuous Testing: Integrate continuous testing into the continuous delivery pipeline, allowing for immediate feedback and quick corrections.

- Risk-Based Testing Approach: Prioritise test cases based on their impact and likelihood, focusing efforts on the areas of highest risk.

2. Case Studies of Successful Implementation of Thorough Testing Protocols

a. Financial Sector: Implementing Agile Testing in Banking Systems
- Context: To counter issues similar to those seen in the Post Office scandal, some banks have moved towards agile testing methodologies, incorporating continuous testing and QA throughout the development process.
- Outcome: This approach has resulted in more reliable banking systems, reduced operational risks, and enhanced customer trust.

b. Healthcare: Electronic Health Records (EHR) System Testing
- Context: The healthcare industry has learnt the importance of exhaustive testing of EHR systems to ensure data accuracy and reliability, given the critical nature of patient information.
- Outcome: Through methodical testing and validation, healthcare providers have minimised errors, improving patient care and operational efficiency.

Best Practices Derived:

- Early and Ongoing Engagement: Engage testers from the onset and throughout the development process, ensuring that testing is an integral part of the software development lifecycle.

- End-User Participation: Involve end-users in the testing process to gather real-world feedback and to better understand how the software will be used in its intended environment.

- Transparency and Accountability: Maintain transparency in reporting test results and establish clear accountability for resolving defects.

The Post Office Horizon Scandal

- Learn from Failures: Implement a culture that learns from mistakes and failures to continually improve testing processes and software quality.

The Post Office Horizon scandal serves as a stark reminder of the consequences of inadequate software testing. By adopting best practices and learning from successful implementations, organisations can avoid similar failures, ensuring software reliability and integrity.

Regulation and Oversight of the post office horizon: Governing Software in Critical Systems

Regulation and oversight in critical software applications, especially within systems as integral as postal services, have become imperative in ensuring reliability, security, and efficiency. The digital transformation of services like the post office introduces complex software systems at the heart of its operations, making their governance a topic of significant concern.

Need for Regulatory Oversight

Reliability: Critical systems require a high degree of reliability since they often support essential services. Regulatory oversight ensures that software systems within the post office meet strict reliability standards to prevent system failures that could disrupt postal services.

Security: With the increasing reliance on digital platforms, the risk of cyber threats looms larger. Regulatory frameworks would enforce stringent security measures to protect sensitive information, including customers' personal data and operational integrity.

Efficiency: Oversight also ensures that software systems are optimised for efficiency, reducing latency, and improving service delivery. It can also encourage the adoption of new technologies, such as AI and blockchain, under a regulated framework to enhance operational capabilities.

Privacy: Regulations can safeguard consumer privacy, particularly important as postal services handle significant amounts of personal data. A regulatory framework would ensure that data handling and processing adhere to privacy laws and ethical standards.

Proposed Frameworks and Guidelines

International Collaboration: Given the global nature of postal services, international regulatory standards and collaborations are crucial. Developing a cohesive set of guidelines that aligns with global standards can help in managing cross-border data flows and services.

Continuous Monitoring and Audit: Implementing continuous monitoring systems for real-time oversight and periodic audits can ensure compliance with set standards and facilitate the early identification of potential issues.

Cybersecurity Standards: Adoption of industry-standard cybersecurity practices and regular security assessments can help in mitigating threats to software systems. This includes encryption, secure coding practices, and vulnerability testing.

Software Reliability Models: Developing and enforcing reliability models specific to critical software in postal systems. These models can help in predicting and improving the reliability and performance of software systems.

Ethical AI Use: As postal services employ more AI-driven solutions, establishing guidelines for the ethical use of AI, including transparency, accountability, and fairness, becomes essential. Regulations should ensure AI systems are explainable and do not introduce bias.

Data Privacy Compliance: Regulatory frameworks must enforce compliance with data protection laws, such as the GDPR in Europe. This includes the principles of data minimisation, consent, and the right to be forgotten.

To conclude, the regulation and oversight of software in critical systems like the post office require a multi-faceted approach that balances innovation with the need for security, reliability, efficiency, and privacy. A well-structured regulatory framework, coupled with international cooperation and adherence to high standards, will be key in governing the horizon of software applications in these essential services.

Rebuilding Trust following the post office horizon scandal: Compensation, Reconciliation, and Reform

Steps Taken by the Post Office to Address the Fallout

1. Public Apology and Acknowledgment: The first and most crucial step involved the Post Office publicly acknowledging the miscarriages of justice and apologising to those affected. This acknowledgment was vital for setting the stage for meaningful compensation and reforms.

2. Independent Reviews and Investigations: The Post Office initiated or cooperated with several independent reviews and inquiries to fully understand the failings and recommend measures

for change. These reviews have been critical in outlining the path forward.

3. Leadership Changes: Recognising that cultural and leadership changes were necessary, the Post Office undertook significant restructuring within its leadership to foster an environment more accountable and sensitive to the needs of its sub-postmasters.

Efforts to Compensate Affected Individuals

1. Compensation Schemes: The Post Office has rolled out compensation schemes aimed at those who were wrongfully convicted and others who suffered financially due to the Horizon system's failings. These schemes aim to offer tangible restitution, although debates about the adequacy and fairness of the compensation continue.

2. Overturning of Wrongful Convictions: A pivotal aspect of the compensation effort involves the legal battles to overturn the wrongful convictions. To date, a significant number of convictions have been quashed, highlighting the journey towards justice for the affected postmasters.

3. Individual Settlements: Besides the broader compensation schemes, there have been efforts to settle with individuals on a case-by-case basis, taking into account the unique aspects of each affected person's situation.

Preventative Measures and Reforms

1. Overhauling the IT System: Critical investments have been made to overhaul and continuously review the IT systems in place, ensuring that the technical flaws that led to the scandal cannot recur.

2. Training and Support for Sub-postmasters: Recognising the need for better support, the Post Office has introduced comprehensive training programs for sub-postmasters, focusing on IT system management, financial handling, and legal support.

3. Regulatory and Oversight Changes: There has been a push for stronger regulatory oversight on the operations of the Post Office, with measures implemented to ensure transparency and accountability are at the forefront of its operations.

4. Cultural Shift: Efforts are underway to foster a culture within the Post Office that values openness,

responsibility, and the well-being of its sub-postmasters. This cultural shift is considered essential for long-term trust rebuilding.

While significant steps have been taken to address the fallout, compensate the affected individuals, and prevent future issues, the journey towards full reconciliation and trust rebuilding is ongoing. The efforts outlined embody a comprehensive approach to rectifying the wrongs of the past, but continuous commitment and vigilance are required to ensure such a scandal is never repeated.

The Future of Software in Public Services following the post office horizon scandal

The Future of Software in Public Services in the aftermath of the Post Office Horizon scandal is a critical sphere of focus, given the profound impact of flawed software systems on public trust and service efficacy. This scandal, which wrongly accused postal workers of financial discrepancies due to errors in the Horizon IT system, has amplified the need for robust, transparent, and accountable software systems within public services. The future direction in this sphere includes several key areas of innovation and improvement.

Innovations and Improvements in Software for Public Services

1. Adoption of Blockchain Technology: Blockchain's inherent characteristics of transparency, immutability, and security make it an ideal candidate for underlying systems in public services.

By creating decentralised and tamper-proof records, blockchain technology can greatly reduce the likelihood of wrongful accusations and enhance trust in public service transactions.

2. AI and Machine Learning for Predictive Analytics: Integrating AI and machine learning for predictive analytics can revolutionise how public services manage data and make decisions. These technologies can identify patterns and forecast potential discrepancies or failures before they escalate, allowing for proactive measures.

3. Human-Centric Design Principles: Ensuring that software systems are designed with the end-user in mind, emphasising usability and accessibility. This approach not only enhances the efficiency and satisfaction of the service but also reduces the chances of operational errors.

4. Robust Testing and Validation Frameworks: Implementing more rigorous testing and validation processes for software before deployment, including real-world scenario testing and validation by independent third parties, to ensure system reliability and accuracy.

5. Incremental and Agile Development: Shifting towards more flexible software development methodologies that allow for regular updates and improvements based on user feedback and evolving needs. This approach facilitates the early detection of issues and makes it easier to implement changes without disrupting the entire system.

The Role of Technology in Enhancing Accountability and Transparency

1. Open Data Initiatives: Promoting transparency by making government data publicly accessible in a comprehensible format, where privacy and security are not compromised. This allows citizens to scrutinise public services and hold them accountable.

2. Digital Ledgers for Financial Transactions: Utilising digital ledgers to record financial transactions in public services can ensure a transparent trail of funds, significantly reducing the risks of errors and fraud.

3. Implementing Software Audits: Regular, independent audits of software systems can ensure they are functioning as intended and highlight any

areas of concern. This practice encourages constant improvement and accountability.

4. Public Participation Platforms: Developing online platforms that enable public participation in decision-making processes can enhance transparency and build trust between citizens and public services.

5. Real-Time Reporting and Monitoring: Establishing systems for real-time reporting and monitoring of public service operations can foster an environment of transparency, where issues can be identified and addressed promptly.

The future of software in public services post-Horizon scandal calls for a broader integration of transparency, accountability, and innovation. Through the adoption of advanced technologies and a commitment to ethical principles, public services can restore public trust and enhance the effectiveness of their operations.

Case Studies: When Software Testing Saved the Day

The Post Office Horizon scandal vividly illustrates the catastrophic consequences of software errors, leading to wrongful convictions, financial ruin, and reputational damage. This episode underscores the indispensable role of thorough software testing. By examining case studies where diligent testing prevented potential disasters, we can distill invaluable lessons for future software development and deployment.

Case Study 1: Mars Climate Orbiter

Background
In 1999, the Mars Climate Orbiter was lost upon entering Mars' atmosphere due to a software error. The engineering team used Imperial units, whereas NASA's specifications called for metric units.

Intervention
This failure highlighted the crucial importance of rigorous testing and verification processes,

particularly in the integration of components from different teams or suppliers.

Lessons
- Consistency in Standards: Ensure all team members follow the same standards and specifications.
- Comprehensive Testing: Implement exhaustive testing scenarios that cover unit, integration, and system testing, with special attention to interfaces and data exchanges.

Case Study 2: Knight Capital Group

Background
In 2012, Knight Capital, a financial services firm, lost $440 million in 45 minutes due to a glitch in its trading software. An unused feature was accidentally reactivated, causing the company to buy high and sell low on 150 different stocks.

Intervention
This incident could have been prevented with more rigorous software testing, specifically testing for latent features and ensuring that old and new systems interact correctly.

Lessons
- Feature Management: Rigorously control and test software features, especially when updating or making changes.
- Risk Assessment: Regularly conduct risk assessments to understand and mitigate potential impacts of software failures.

Case Study 3: Boeing 737 MAX

Background
The Boeing 737 MAX experienced two catastrophic crashes in 2018 and 2019, largely attributed to the Manoeuvring Characteristics Augmentation System (MCAS). This software was inadequately tested and relied on a single angle of attack (AOA) sensor.

Intervention
A comprehensive review and overhaul of the MCAS system were undertaken, with an emphasis on extensive testing under various scenarios, including sensor failures.

Lessons
- Redundancy and Fail-safes: Ensure critical systems have redundant checks and fail-safe mechanisms.

- Stakeholder Involvement: Involve all stakeholders, including end-users, in the testing process to gather a broad range of perspectives and scenarios.

Conclusion

These case studies demonstrate the vital importance of comprehensive and rigorous software testing in averting disasters. Key lessons include the need for consistency in standards, thorough feature management, dedicated risk assessments, ensuring redundancy and fail-safes, and involving all stakeholders in the testing process. These strategies can help prevent the kind of outcomes seen in the Post Office Horizon scandal, turning potential crises into stories of averted disaster.

A Call for Ethical Software Development and Testing following the post office horizon scandal

The Post Office Horizon scandal remains a poignant reminder of the catastrophic consequences when ethics in software development and rigorous testing are overlooked. This incident underlines the critical need for integrity, accountability, and thoroughness in creating and implementing technological systems. The victims of this scandal faced immense personal, financial, and emotional turmoil, underscoring the human cost of technological oversights.

Key Lessons from the Horizon Scandal:
1. Accountability: Software developers and the organisations deploying technology must be held accountable for the systems they implement. This involves ensuring that there is a clear

understanding of the impact these systems can have on people's lives and livelihoods.

2. Ethical Considerations: Ethical principles should guide the development and deployment of software. This includes considering the potential impacts on all stakeholders and ensuring that systems do not unfairly prejudice any group.

3. Rigorous Testing: Comprehensive testing is crucial before and after the deployment of technological systems. Such testing should not only focus on system functionality but also on its real-world impact on users.

4. Transparency and Dialogue: There must be an open channel of communication between developers, users, and regulatory bodies. Feedback loops are essential for identifying and addressing issues promptly.

5. Education and Awareness: Educating developers about the ethical implications of their work can foster a culture of responsibility. Similarly, educating users about their rights and the functionality of the systems they interact with is vital.

Envisioning a Future of Ethical Software Development and Testing:
The future of software development and testing must be rooted in a foundation of ethical standards

and rigorous methodologies. In this envisioned future, technology serves humanity positively, enhancing lives without infringing on rights or causing harm. Developers and organisations work transparently, prioritising the well-being and privacy of individuals over profit or efficiency.

Ethical boards or committees, comprised of developers, ethicists, and laypersons, should oversee the implementation of new technologies, ensuring that ethical considerations are at the forefront of every decision. Continuous education on the ethical use of technology for developers and users alike will elevate the collective understanding and application of technology for the greater good.

The Post Office Horizon scandal teaches us that technology's potential to benefit society is immense, but so is its potential to harm when neglected ethically and not rigorously tested. By learning from these mistakes, the future of software development can be one where technology uplifts and protects, ensuring that such a scandal never recurs. Ensuring the ethical development and testing of software is not just a technical necessity but a moral imperative to prevent the repetition of past mistakes and to protect society's most vulnerable members.

Foundations of Scrum Agile
Education

£2.99

App Store

Google Play

The Post Office Horizon Scandal

Agile Development with DevOps

Agile Project Management: Navigating Pros and Cons of Scrum, Kanban and combining them

Air Traffic Control & Baggage Handling: A Kanban Story

Communication Troubles of a Scrum Team

Disney's FastPass: A Queue Story

Imperative of Software Testing: The Post Office Horizon Scandal

Introducing the Douglass Model for Agile Coaches

Kaizen: The Philosophy of Continuous Improvement for Business and Education

Mastering Software Quality Assurance: A Comprehensive Guide

McDonald's: A Kanban Story

Nightclub Entry Token System: A Kanban Story

Pizza Delivery: A Kanban Story

Scrum: Unveiling the Agile Method

Testing SaaS: A Comprehensive Guide to Software Testing for Cloud-Based Applications

The Agile Way to Fitness: Achieving fitness goals for IT professionals

The Art of Lean: Production Systems and Marketing Strategies in the modern era

The Post Office Horizon Scandal

The Art of Waterfall: A Traditional Approach to Project Management

The Board: A day-to-day feel of life on a Kanban team

The Sprint: A day-to-day feel of life on a Scrum team

The Whole Game: Systems Thinking Approach to Invasion Sports

Traffic Light System: A Kanban Story

www.ingramcontent.com/pod-product-compliance
Lightning Source LLC
LaVergne TN
LVHW051615050326
832903LV00033B/4518

*9 7 9 8 3 2 3 7 9 0 2 1 0 *